*For Kelly Colasanti;*

*Be:*

# poetic
# license

# *Confirmed*

*N. Clt*

## Neil E. Clement

*Copyright © 2014 Neil E. Clement.*

*All rights reserved. No part of this book may be reproduced, stored, or transmitted by any means – whether auditory, graphic, mechanical, or electronic – without written permission of both publisher and author, except in the case of brief excerpts used in critical articles and reviews. Unauthorized reproduction of any part of this work is illegal and is punishable by law.*

*This is a work of fiction. Names, characters, places and incidents are products of the author's imagination. Any and all characters and locations appearing in this work are purely fictitious. Any resemblance to actual events or locales or real persons, living or dead, is entirely coincidental with the following exceptions:*

"Be the ball." from *Caddyshack;* "Sufferin' succotash!", "What a Maroon!", "What's Up, Doc?" and "That's all folks!" from *Looney Tunes* / Warner Brothers; "Play it again, Sam." from *Casablanca;* "Just the facts, ma'am." from *Dragnet;* "I'm a doctor, Jim, not a tomato.", "Belay that order!", "I'm givin' it all she's got, Cap'n!" and "Beam me up." from *Star Trek;* "Up, up and away!" from *Superman;* "Neverland" from *Peter Pan.* These sources are gratefully acknowledged with only the greatest respect and admiration.

*Cover Content & Cover Photography Copyright © 2014 by MTCC Publishing Company LLC, All Rights Reserved.*

*Cover Design by Michael Faulk*

*ISBN: 978-0-9895378-7-2 (sc)*

*ISBN: 978-0-9895378-8-9 (e)*

# MTCC Publishing Company LLC

www.mtccpc.com

I dedicate this book with great affection to my brothers and sisters:

Robert Marshall, the Elder

Mary Lynn, the Nurturer

Johnny Lee, the Musician

Marsha Jeanne, the Muse

Marshall William, the Traveler

Nancy Rae Follis, the Younger

May we never lose touch completely.

## Table of Contents

| | |
|---|---|
| Go!| 1 |
| Love the Children| 3 |
| Paradise| 5 |
| Here!| 7 |
| Spring| 9 |
| Feelings| 11 |
| Tears| 13 |
| Stings| 15 |
| Get Up!| 17 |
| Dirty Dishes| 19 |
| Cobwebs| 21 |
| Morning| 23 |
| Oops!| 25 |
| Easy there!| 27 |
| See the Sea| 29 |
| Connections| 31 |
| Skepticism| 33 |
| Drumbeats| 37 |
| Night and Day| 39 |
| Change| 41 |
| Crawl| 43 |
| Wonder!| 45 |
| Create| 47 |
| Be!| 49 |
| Suspense!| 51 |
| Seeds| 53 |
| Escape!| 55 |
| Wait!| 57 |
| Lies| 59 |
| Moods| 61 |
| Infinity| 63 |

## Go!

to know is to go
to be, to do
to know is to show
that you can too

to know is to see
all that can be
to know is not free
not plucked from tree

to know is to go
to be, to do
to know is to show
that you can too

to know is to make
things real, not fake
to know is to estimate
take chance on mistake

to know is to go
to be, to do
to know is to show
that you can too

so go, not slow, make haste
the time one must not waste
the only way you'll get a taste
is to get in line and participaste!

How do you know when you say something that you are not just repeating something that has already been said?

The path to enlightenment is more of a multi-lane super highway with many, many entrances and exits and not very many legible signs. Avoid potholes and low bridges.

To see or not to see, that is the key, to your ability, to be what you want to be.

## Love the Children

what's gon' happen is gon' happen
an' it don' make no nevermind
whether you see or start toe tappin'

spare the rod and love the child
you will find that none go wild
spare the rod and love the child

what's gon' go is gon' go
an' it don' always move that slow
stand still and get runned ohvah

spare the rod and love the child
you will find that none go wild
spare the rod and love the child

what's gon' be is gon' be
an' it don' matta much to me
frettin' not gon' make you free

spare the rod and love the child
you will find that none go wild
spare the rod and love the child

True Friendship can never be taken from you but it can be lost.

True Love Cannot Harm. True Love Grows in Strength and Gives Strength in Equal Proportions.

The love that is true makes the strongest glue.

**Paradise**

who, who are you?
make some noise, break on through
shed your shell
pop that cocoon
the future waits, and none too soon

what, what can I do?
to otherwise convince you
destiny melding past with next
be what you want to be
let none that be sway thee

when, when will we know?
how, how can we grow?
our paradise slips away
each and every day
best we amend our ways

where, oh where can we be?
floating through this galaxy
timeflow outpacing speeding space
far beyond our periphery
we who can see to eternity

why, why, am I?
here today, tomorrow shy
isn't it obvious?
can't you see?
the breathing of reality

The problem with acquiring things is now you have to take care of them.

---

As passengers on this our Ark in the Dark, we are but passing through Airport Earth. Responsible travelers leave their space cleaner than they found it and show kindness to other passengers.

---

As the first day since yesterday and the last day before tomorrow, today is by far the best day to do whatever needs to be done.

**Here!**

into the void we cast our toil
message sent by interstellar foil
we are here! with all we hold dear!
wishing we knew who is who
inquisitive through and through

trees of life branching out
*everywhere*, without a doubt
blessed redundance breeding abundance
racing sparks kiss fading quarks
cosmos filled with beating hearts

emerging from the veil of dreams
mysterious dimensions roaming free
particle physics prescribe the limits
stretching space to make a place
eternity grants unpredictable fates

When you do your part to make a positive difference the human race can reach a new magnificence.

Fair weather friends generally sail away on the first ill wind.

If you think you know something it's a sure sign you don't.

## Spring

green shoots emerge from dormant ground
without a whisper; they make no sound
each tiny sprout comes around
where sunlight strikes; there life is found

send in the bees please
to pollinate the plums and peas
to propagate all the plants and trees
with flowers that reach out and tease

spring has sprung; there's no holding back
nature's bounty fills every niche and crack
algae blooms darken ocean water feeding the pack
slumbering northland awakens without any slack

send in the bees please
to pollinate the plums and peas
to propagate all the plants and trees
with flowers that reach out and tease

Beauty is a form of radiation.

---

Life. Cooked up by Mother Nature using all natural ingredients. This much we know. On the flipside, not only do we not know where she found the recipe, we can't even determine if it is an original or a copy.

---

Our true loyalty belongs to those yet to come.

**Feelings**

when you are down and feeling blue
something must have come unglued
let these feelings slide on through
free yourself of thoughts undue

lest others see just how you feel
when eye to eye you try to deal
and your mask does not conceal
what you know or should reveal

feelings can and should add spice
but offer no real good advice
some are fleeting, some entice
for best results use only nice

Disappointment is the constant companion of those who wait for others to do for them what they could be doing for themselves.

A Lasting Impression left by an Unforgettable Experience or a Burning Emotion can and does color all decisions made afterwards.

Broken hearts can often be mended using sticky teardrops.

**Tears**

once the cap is off the pen
from the tip should words flow again
give it a try; you may begin

take notice and give a care
the world is shrinking in despair
as we dominate the biosphere

all the rhinos almost gone
horns of plenty now are done
all for nothing; we leave none

whales beach themselves; message clear
oceans once pristine are smeared
dry eyes no more; just filled with tears

If you do only one thing today let it be an act of kindness.

I'm gonna go with reality. Unreality is more than I'm willing to deal with right now.

As we go about recording history we have to ask ourselves how we can explain to future generations not just why certain groups or even individuals were allowed to manipulate the population at large into making often grotesque and *extremely* expensive far-reaching mistakes in general policy causing many unnecessary planetary-wide problems but more importantly we must explain why the majority was unable to prevent this decidedly inappropriate behavior from happening repeatedly in the first place.

**Stings**

time melts away
doesn't want to stay
who can say? why today?

thoughts fly without wings
ideas emerge from deepest dreams
leaving little to which memory clings

can we say we hold sway?
as we watch nature play
our world not ours to fray

of all the things that each day brings
tune into the song in your heartstrings
to stay aware, to avoid many stings

The totality of our reality makes the 46 billion linear light year distance to the edge of the observable universe the equivalent of no more than a few hundred ticks on an infinite cosmic ruler. Still, this gives us a lot to work with.

The mind has its own built-in software for filtering memories. Some things we remember and some things we don't. I can easily recall vivid images of Lois Lane, Clark Kent, Jimmy Olsen & Perry White from 50 years ago but what I had for breakfast last week is rather vague. Thank goodness nature included this feature.

Your assignment today, should you choose to accept it, is to read the lyrics of *Imagine* by John Lennon, then "Imagine all the people, Sharing all the world", and not just with each other, but especially with ALL other life. This message will self-destruct in five centuries.

**Get Up!**

day is dawning
night is yawning
oceans teeming
life is spawning

get up, get up
the light is bright
get up, get up
and see the sight

birds are singing
songs are winging
skies teeming
lives are mingling

get up, get up
put feet on ground
get up, get up
and hear the sound

hunger pangs
activate fangs
farmlands teeming
must give thanks

get up, get up
coffee will help
get up, get up
and cherish the smell

taste and touch
round out the bunch
sixth sense too
don't ignore that hunch

get up, get up
the fat's in the fire
get up, get up
and be inspired

Happiness will be yours the moment you embrace it and will stick around for as long as you continue to do so.

---

You will not notice when you cross the line from confidence to conceit but your friends will.

---

"From whence does inspiration arise?" asks the novice, as if anyone says 'whence' anymore.
"From within" replied the sage.
"Within what?" the novice meekly inquires.
"From within your deepest desires" sayeth the sage, even though no one says 'sayeth' anymore either.
"Good to know" speaketh the novice.

**Dirty Dishes**

dirty dishes in the sink
can't ignore; can't seem to think
must wash up before they stink

dirty dishes in the sink
no room to even take a drink
no silverware left to stir or clink

dirty dishes in the sink
still there no matter how much I blink
the washing hose must have a crink

dirty dishes in the sink
accumulate; can't sleep a wink
use soapy water; the pile will shrink

Life is a river like the Amazon, endlessly flowing vast amounts of fresh water into an exponentially vaster cosmic ocean; initially making a big impact but ultimately getting completely absorbed by the larger volume and leaving little trace. Just ask anyone living three hundred million years ago.

～

While the size of the fish does matter, it is the size of the ripples it leaves behind that actually gets more attention.

～

100% Earth. Machine Wash Cold With Like Color.
Color May Bleed. Tumble Dry Low.
Do Not Iron Or Dry Clean If Decorated. Do Not Bleach.
For Best Results Take Only That Which Can Be Replaced.

**Cobwebs**

got rain on the brain
thoughts flowing down the drain
must be some way to refrain

something really good might slip away
sometimes to resurface another day
must have something important to say

clouds are fogging up my vision
sunshine hiding made by fusion
must lose cobwebs, lose confusion

reaching out, contact made
now can experience trade?
must be life, must not fade

New data strongly suggests that 95% of our universe is completely undetectable.
I'm not sure which is more amazing, the knowledge that the bulk of our reality is entirely invisible, or the fact that we were able to figure this out.

---

It may seem obvious that Time stands still for no one but there really is no way to actually prove this just yet.
Who doesn't love a good mystery?

---

The ability to formulate and process random thoughts randomly is rooted in the quite orderly array of cells making up nature's masterpiece: our biological brain. Here's a thought:

Our resources are dwindling as our population is exploding, some populations more than others.

We should try to realistically imagine what the world will be like in 100 years and guide our actions accordingly. It might be prudent to plan on keeping the planet habitable and maintaining the diversity of life we have today. We should give it a try!

## Morning

night numbs neatly
chicken cackles completely
sun shines sweetly

day dissolves dreams
thoughts trade teams
coffee curdles creams

children calling collectively
people playing positively
crows cawing conclusively

billygoats braying bountifully
morning memories mystically
world unwinding wonderfully

Paying too much attention to any one problem sends an open invitation to many others to come and visit.

When watching TV turn the audio off and you will see many things that once escaped your notice.

We interrupt your regularly scheduled programming to bring you this special announcement. Alert: The fungus lobby has declared that shoes were invented to boost sales of antifungal ointment. They believe credit should be given where credit is due. The shoe lobby issued an official "no comment" statement. The foot lobby declined to step into this debate.

**Oops!**

petted the cat
rubbed my eye
oops, shouldn't a aught'a done that

was late for chat
gas pedal lay flat
oops, shouldn't a aught'a done that

checked a plug
used a slug
oops, shouldn't a aught'a done that

no instructions to read
but still did i do the deed
oops, shouldn't a aught'a done that

many things can go wrong
many things can go right
the thing to remember is

one can't really be in a bad way
unless one is unable to say
oops, shouldn't a aught'a done that

Reflecting on what has been and what could be will define your sense of purpose.

Success in life is directly proportional to one's ability to eliminate unnecessary distractions.

Align your moral compass to automatically attract quality emotive experiences while simultaneously repelling any and all disadvantageous thoughts. Leave room for wild and crazy ideas to energize those artistic moments when inspiration strikes. Flexibility will be your key to success.

**Easy there!**

Be sensible.
Use your head.
Remain calm.
Stay the course.
Stay cool.
As you were.
At ease!
Enough is enough.
Be the ball.
Go for it.
What a maroon!
What's up, Doc?
Just add water.
Play it again, Sam.
Just the facts, ma'am.
I'm a doctor, Jim, not a tomato.
Full speed ahead.
Call for backup.
Signal the fleet.
United we stand.
Belay that order!
I'm givin' it all she's got, Cap'n!
Up, up and away!
Watch your back.
Watch your step.
That's all folks!
Beam me up.

Finding one's inner self means one must first lose it.

Personality is forged in the crucible of experience.

It would be unrealistic to expect to hit the ball out of the park every time the chance presents itself.
Fortunately for us, Boundless Optimism does not recognize this limitation.

## See the Sea

we need the sea, you see
the only place on earth
where food, water and air
are all produced for free

the sea needs us, you see
to stop dumping our waste
else water no more, just paste

we need the sea, you see
enormous engine of life
land created and disposed
nature made with no recurring fee

the sea needs us, you see
to stop dumping our waste
else water no more, just paste

we need the sea, you see
here is where we will find the key
unlocking our potential to be
star travelers exploring the galaxy

the sea needs us, you see
to stop dumping our waste
else water no more, just paste

billions of years did it take
this opportunity of ours to make
foolish would we be to forsake
this chance we have to investigate

How much you know defines how far you go.

Look no further than the end of your nose if Neverland is where you wish to go.

You will learn the most by being open and receptive to new ideas.

**Connections**

study hard and you will find
bits of knowledge in your mind
useful only when combined
in the right way, in the right time

it is for you to do
as the de facto CPU
to crunch the data, to see what's new

listen close and you can hear
completed thoughts as they near
great ideas bursting clear
mindfog fading to the rear

it is for you to do
as the de facto CPU
to crunch the data, to see what's new

study hard and you will see
that being all you can be
is not easy, is not free
but is definitely well worth the fee

it is for you to do
as the de facto CPU
to crunch the data, to see what's new

and if by chance you make the grade
there comes a time you will be paid
how much depends on how you made
those connections in your mind each day

Consisting of only faint bioelectrical impulses, and possessing virtually no actual substance at all, thoughts can be used to overcome practically any obstacle.

Reality™ powered by Existence™ is really nothing more than what you think it is.

You can go or you can stay. You are just as likely to get somewhere either way.

## Skepticism

Are you joking?
Are you mad?
Are you for real?
Are you serious?
Are you sure?
Beg pardon?
But... But... But...
Can't be!
Can this be?
Come again?
Come off it!
Come on!
For the love of _____! (Usually Pete)
For _____ sake!    (Also usually Pete)
For real?
Get away!
Get off it!
Get off with you!
Get outta here!
Get real!
Gimme the latest lowdown!
Gimme the real deal!
Go on!
Good Golly Miss Molly!
Goodness!
Good grief!
Goodness sake!
Gracious!
Good gracious!
Great Goobly Gumdrops!
Have you gone bananas?
Have you gone crackers?
Have you gone loco?

Have you gone 'round the bend?
Have you lost it?
How can it be?
How is that possible?
How's that?
How in the world...?
I can't believe it!
Is that for real?
Is that for sure?
Is that the real skinny?
Is that right?
Is that so?
Is that the straight scoop?
Is that on the up and up?
Is that the unvarnished truth?
It can't be!
It just can't be!
It's not possible!
Oh, my!
Uh oh!
Oh no!
Oh well.
No kidding?
No!!!
No foolin'?
No phony baloney?
No way!
No way, no how!
Not happenin'!
Really?
Say again?
Say it ain't so!
Say what?
Say you don't mean it!
Seriously?
Shush now.
Sounds pretty fishy!
Sufferin' succotash!

# Poetic License Confirmed

That right?
That so?
That can't be right!
That's absurd!
That's ridiculous!
There's no mistake?
There's no way!
Too much!
Truthfully?
Well, shut my mouth wide open!
Well, I'll be dipped in _____!
What the...?
What planet are you from?
You ain't lyin'?
You are certain?
You've gotta be kidding!
You don't mean it!
You don't say!
You must be daft!
You must be kidding!
You must be joking!
You joshin' me?
You must be delirious!
You must be mistaken!
You pullin' my leg?
You really think so?
You're not funnin'?
You're not serious!
You can't be serious.
You yankin' my chain?

Tomorrow does come.  It just seems like today.

---

If you want to get ahead some things will have to be left behind.

---

Exponential growth of any given problem is easily achieved simply by ignoring it.

**Drumbeats**

in drifting dreams we bend
reality, as shifting shadows send
new ideas, which need to blend
with old ideas; mix up the trend

can you truly hear?
the drumbeats as they near
thoughts clicking into gear
live your life, lose your fear!

silent souls sailing to the light
flying free and free of fright
weirding wolves wailing in the night
their message clear: embrace our birthright

can you truly hear?
the drumbeats as they near
thoughts clicking into gear
live your life, lose your fear!

people do and people say
not always in the same way
you can pass or you can stay
unfunny games that people play

can you truly hear?
the drumbeats as they near
thoughts clicking into gear
live your life, lose your fear!

If you are on schedule to meet a schedule then maybe you should schedule a break.

The future is now.  This is it.  Handle it.

The only real mystery is why there needs to be one.

## Night and Day

earth go round, sun go down
moon rise up, starshine unstuck

hail the night, time of light
galaxy glow, soft as snow

quiet falls on sleeping dolls
dreams unfold, future untold

hail the night, time of light
galaxy glow, soft as snow

morning comes, bang the drums
wake the world, thoughts unfurl

hail the day, time to play
sunshine bright, hide the night

be true to you, this must you do
life beckons, time reckons

hail the day, time to play
sunshine bright, hide the night

Knowledge does not bestow wisdom but is a required element in the periodic table of understanding.

If you wish to find answers you must see beyond tomorrow.

It is far more difficult to ask the right question than it is to find the correct answer.

**Change**

in restless dreams we see
visions past and things to be
shining mirrors in the mind
reflecting riddles to unwind

come closer now to hear the tale
of knowledge lost and ignorance haled
for a thousand years mankind was stalled
when Alexandria burned through broken walls

we must each of us never forget
that dark will rule when reason has fled
good men must stand when evil speaks
wise people engage when policy reeks

we know the things we need to do
to make sure wrongs are righted true
the people looking back on tomorrow
deserve no sad tidings nor our sorrow

pretend now that it doesn't matter
and watch the people as they scatter
what we leave is what we take
our children we must not forsake

days unfold; events unfurl
endless change the only rule
what we give is what we make
a world where all may educate

You can only know something if you have something else to compare it to.

⁂

Only now is the Age of True Enlightenment with vast amounts of data at our fingertips for the asking. Great Power will be wielded by anyone properly interrogating this growing knowledge base.
Whomever has the best interface controlling the fastest computer system with access to the most data and asking pertinent questions will have a natural advantage over all others in most endeavors. The Age of Anonymity has come to an end. This seems like Something We Should Care About.

⁂

The need to succeed can breed greed. Take heed. Leave everything else.

**Crawl**

i spied a spider on the wall
it really wasn't very tall
it was in fact rather small

how cool it is how spidey can crawl
upside down without a fall
just eight spindly legs poking out of a ball

i left it there in the hall
its food nearby, no doubt at all
it made no move, as i recall

it made a haul with brazen gall
then disappeared without a stall
no trace can now be seen a 'tall

Where you came from is not nearly as important as where you are going.

Say not I cannot; say only why not?

Good assistants overcome resistance using persistence.

**Wonder!**

the mind is blind
until it can find
some data to grind
it loves to unwind
information sublime

thoughts split asunder
ideas reverberate like thunder
knowledge: nature made plunder
yours if you let yourself wonder

the mind is blind
until it can find
some data to grind
it loves to unwind
information sublime

free thinking is your gift
letting memories shapeshift
if you want to get the drift
all the data must you sift

the mind is blind
until it can find
some data to grind
it loves to unwind
information sublime

the notions that we carry
beliefs to which we marry
of these must we be wary
an open mind most necessary

The only really useful advice is that which comes from within oneself.

Each of us is actually two people, one whom we really are and one whom we think we are.

Local gravitational effects can cause the direction of a volume of fluid in motion to default to the path of least resistance. When gravity is not present a volume of fluid becomes an amorphous blob subject to Newton's laws of motion. Do not let the gravity of this situation escape you.

**Create**

have you heard the news??
the future is yours to use
in any way you choose
you can snooze or get good reviews
the choice is yours to bruise

get on with it then
make something out of nothing again
if nothing else pretend
as good a place as any to begin
creativity has no boundaries my friend

There is within each of us one thing we really excel at. Identify this trait in yourself and pursue it assiduously to maximize your life potential.

Informative Impressions can be generated by data mining memories. Move swiftly through these images and resist the temptation to dwell in any one place for longer than 3 seconds.

Success can be yours with a little careful planning.

**Be!**

at break of day
dreams go astray
beams of light
free the night

be free
be key
be thee
to see

rouse sluggish thoughts
douse yourself or not
watch fate cast your lot
each day become fine art

be free
be key
be thee
to see

resist the urge
when others merge
let independence surge
as nerve feeds courage

be free
be key
be thee
to see

Trueness can be seen only by mastering the art of reflection.

The beauty of beauty is that it can be anything you want it to be.

Possessions give you something to do. Thoughts give you somewhere to go.
Go somewhere and do something. No reason not to.

**Suspense!**

firelight flickers in deep of night
shadows dance with sheer delight

could be friend, could be foe
best go slow until you know

now is not the time to shout
at least until you have found out

who is there and who is not
what is real and what is naught

move like a whisper, quiet as can be
get close up, the better to see
are any marshmallows being roasted for me?

Being in harmony with your background is the surest way to avoid attention.

⁂

Those who refuse to get involved are not entitled to express an opinion.

⁂

You can only truly know something if you figured it out for yourself on your own.

## Seeds

there was a young lad from McBumble
whose uncanny ability was to stumble
onto places so grand he only could mumble
boundless beauty made breathlessly humble

it is we who can see
others must there be
seeds of life spread for free
cosmos reaching for infinity

mountains kissing sky can crumble
water falling into ultrasonic rumble
earth spins round sun all a-tumble
stars shine everywhere in a vast jumble

it is we who can see
others must there be
seeds of life spread for free
cosmos reaching for infinity

it is for us to do
to fly the ark, to brave the boo
else the ball we fumble
leaving none who may grumble

Wisdom comes only to those who know they don't have any.

Choose or be chosen, the choice is yours.

If at first you fail to see, try, and try, but don't look at me.

**Escape!**

the world that we know has not always been so
it changes itself on the go, reforming ever so slow

the whole globe once was flat with not even a gnat
with no mountains, no valleys, and no moon to look at

no water could be seen, no air held a sheen
just boiling land everywhere; magma was king

how different it appears after billions of years and oceans of tears
this astonishing ball of rock majestically circling our star so near

so massive and so fragile our planet of light, now chock full of life
but we stand on the brink of events that many think will bring strife

one chance we have to get it right, to explore the stars of the night
petty squabbles must be set aside if we really wish to make the flight

Our most advanced viewing apparatuses tell us that only 5% of the stuff in this universe is 'visible'.

The biological viewing sense we have been gifted with can only detect a very, very small amount of this 5%.

The actual percentage of the amount of light visible to humans in the entire electromagnetic spectrum is a ridiculously small number.

Our own senses, all six of them including time-sense, actually tell us very little of this place where we live.

Practically everything in our universe is either too big or too small for us to be able to perceive directly.

This means that just about everything of any actual significance is invisible to us.

And yet, up until the beginning of the twentieth century, virtually all of the accumulated knowledge of the human race was developed within this miniscule frame of reference.

One has no choice but to wonder just how accurate any conclusions, customs or traditions derived from this incredibly narrow perspective can possibly be.

One must wonder.

**Wait!**

pronto?
but wait
don't go
one sec
can you hold?
one mo
just a sec
can I put you on hold?
una momento
one moment
hold on
one second
half a mo!
give me a minute
look here
hold everything!
I'll be right back
one minute, if you please
back in a jiffy
hold the fort
please hold
hold please
a moment, please!
thank you for your patience
leave a message at the beep

If you want to make some money, you're prob'ly gonna hav'ta spend some money.

There are no taxes, only income relief.

Authority is just another word for nonaccountable.

**Lies**

the truth, the truth, gimme the truth
but why, why, why can't I lie?
the truth is you can lie if you try
you can be sly, deny, defy and decry
you can speak your best ad lib
and weave a big whopping fib
you might even believe
the things you conceive
you might even deceive
yourself in your need
but this you must concede
one lie is never enough
the truth is just too tough
no lie can stand alone
it needs others to enjoin
lies multiply like coins
but as you spin your web
this thought keep in your head
your chances are quite slim
that others will buy in
you might succeed at first
then will your bubble burst
and you will come off worst
telling no lies not always easy to do
but works much the best for me and for you

The ruling elite should not exist in a government supposedly run by consensus.

Thoughts are free. What you do with them may not be.

Car trouble. Stay tuned to this station for further announcements. In the event of an actual emergency, please handle it.

## Moods

'twas once a young lass from k'Noot
whose choice it was to play flute
'bout this was she quite resolute
a decision proved most astute
as practice gave skill absolute

her tones would gently melt the air
and make you cry in your despair
or lift you up beyond compare
her music was her gift to share
the love you feel already there

nimble fingers weave the mood
barely breathing comes the tune
softly lilting through the room
sprouting wings that afternoon
to fly away and race the moon

her tones would gently melt the air
and make you cry in your despair
or lift you up beyond compare
her music was her gift to share
the love you feel already there

none can say just how she knew
how to play such magic muse
but all agree she lit the fuse
and now we have such daring do
as all the great composers fugue

The music of the universe can only be heard when one is tuned to the right wavelength.

Imagination: brainchild of Inspiration; fed by Desire. Comes only to those who really need it.

Whether you do or you don't is hardly the point; what matters is how hard you try.

## Infinity

how far is that star out thar?
to go to the glow you must know
sift the gift of the redshift
trust true blue coming at you

fly beyond the sky
just say goodbye
fly beyond the sky
destiny forever shy

our home on loan now grown
too small for all to crawl
space beckons, time reckons
life delivers no seconds

fly beyond the sky
just say goodbye
fly beyond the sky
destiny forever shy

to stay is to pay someday
far too much only to touch
infinity staring back at me
go now, fly, be free, be free

Isn't It Annoying How This Comment Ruins a Perfectly Good Blank Page?